BURNS

ELAINE LANDAU

Marshall Cavendish
Benchmark
New York

Expert Reader: Stuart E. Beeber, MD, Chappaqua Pediatrics, Chappaqua, NY

Published by Marshall Cavendish Benchmark.
An imprint of Marshall Cavendish Corporation

Other Marshall Cavendish Offices:
Marshall Cavendish International (Asia) Private Limited, 1 New Industrial Road, Singapore 536196 • Marshall Cavendish International (Thailand) Co Ltd. 253 Asoke, 12th Flr, Sukhumvit 21 Road, Klongtoey Nua, Wattana, Bangkok 10110, Thailand • Marshall Cavendish (Malaysia) Sdn Bhd, Times Subang, Lot 46, Subang Hi-Tech Industrial Park, Batu Tiga, 40000 Shah Alam, Selangor Darul Ehsan, Malaysia

Marshall Cavendish is a trademark of Times Publishing Limited
All websites were available and accurate when this book was sent to press.

Library of Congress Cataloging-in-Publication Data
Landau, Elaine.
Burns / by Elaine Landau.
p. cm. — (Head-to-toe health)
Includes index.
Summary: "Provides basic information about the different types of burns a person can get, as well as how to prevent them."—Provided by publisher.
   ISBN 978-0-7614-4832-7
   1. Burns and scalds—Juvenile literature. 2. Skin—Wounds and injuries—Juvenile literature. I. Title.
   RD96.4.L33 2010
   617.1'1—dc22
   2009031495

Editor: Joy Bean
Publisher: Michelle Bisson
Art Director: Anahid Hamparian
Series Designer: Alex Ferrari

Photo research by Candlepants Incorporated.

Cover Photo: Ralf Nau / Getty Images.

The photographs in this book are used by permission and through the courtesy of: *Alamy Images*: imagebroker, 4; Cultura, 6; John Miller, 9; Chris Howes/Wild Places Photography, 10; WoodyStock, 11; Richard Levine, 18. *Corbis:* Thom Lang, 7; Joel W. Rogers, 16. *Getty Images*: Dan Bigelow, 8; Peter Cade, 13; Simon Watson, 15; Tim Platt, 19; Kay Blaschke, 20; Jupiterimages, 23; ShalomOrmsby, 24; Steven Puetzer, 25.

Printed in Malaysia(T)
1 3 5 6 4 2

CONTENTS

You Took a Chance

You just came home from playing in the snow. You're all ready for a cup of hot chocolate. Your mother isn't home, but you've seen her make hot chocolate many times. You decide to try it yourself. To start, you heat up a cup of water in the microwave.

Just as the microwave beeps, the phone rings. You know it's a friend from school, and you really want to talk to her. But the hot water is ready, and you don't want cold chocolate.

You don't see the oven mitt. You need the mitt to take the cup out of the microwave safely. But the cup has only been heating for a few minutes, and you figure it can't be that hot. Besides, you don't want to miss your phone call.

You take a chance and reach for the cup with your bare hands. That was a mistake. The moment you touch the cup, you know it. OUCH! You've burned your fingers!

◀ **More than 200 million microwave ovens are used around the world. You can prepare a meal in minutes with a microwave. But you must use these ovens with care.**

Right away, you drop the cup. As it falls to the floor, the hot water splashes on your legs. Now your legs are **scalded**, too. It all happened in less than five seconds. The burns really hurt. You missed your phone call, too, but that doesn't seem to matter now.

It's never smart to trade safety for speed, but people of all ages do it. Burns are common among children. Every day thousands of kids visit emergency rooms to get burns treated. Sometimes they have to stay in the hospital. Some have even lost their lives in fires or due to serious burns.

In this book you'll learn that there are different kinds of burns. You'll also learn how burns are treated. Best of all, you'll get tips on how to avoid being burned. So read on—and stay safe!

**Question: What's better than using one oven mitt?
Answer: Using two!**

DID YOU KNOW?

Burns caused by hot water and steam are the
most common burns among young children. These burns can
be very dangerous. Young children have thinner skin than older kids
and grown-ups. This means their skin burns at lower temperatures,
and it also burns more deeply. So it's really important for
kids to be extra careful!

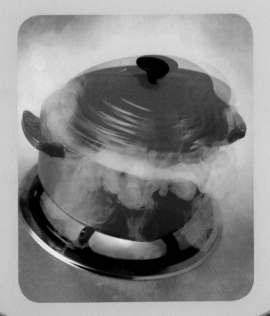

BURNS ARE BAD NEWS

It's going to be a great day. You and your friends are headed to the beach. You have to take your little brother along, but you don't mind. He listens to you most of the time.

Today isn't one of those times, though. After you get to the beach, your brother refuses to put on sunscreen. He says it's too greasy.

This boy is smiling because he's put on sunscreen and he knows he's safe to play in the sun.

Your brother spends the day unprotected from the sun. You think his skin is turning a little red, but he says he's fine. As it turns out, he's not fine at all.

By evening, his skin looks beet red. He looks like a human lobster. His skin is hot when you touch it. He says it hurts a lot, too. Your brother is seriously sunburned.

NOT ALL BURNS ARE THE SAME

Did you know that there are different levels of burns? Some burns are worse than others. It all depends on how many layers of skin are damaged. The deeper the burn, the more serious it is.

A first-degree burn is the mildest (least serious) burn. That doesn't mean first-degree burns don't hurt—they do! In a first-degree burn, only the epidermis—the top layer of skin that we can see—gets damaged. A mild sunburn is an example of a first-degree burn.

In a first-degree burn the burned area gets red and might be a bit puffy.

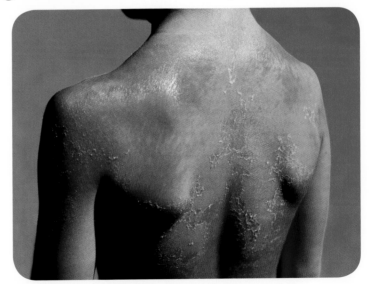

A bad sunburn can be very painful. Yet most of these burns can be prevented.

Often the skin over the burned area peels off after a couple of days. First-degree burns usually heal in three to six days.

Second-degree burns are more serious than first-degree burns. These burns reach deeper into the skin. They damage both the epidermis and the dermis—the layer of skin below the epidermis. Second-degree burns are more painful than first-degree burns. They take longer to heal, too.

If you get a second-degree burn, blisters may form. The blisters are filled with a watery liquid called serum. The fluid-filled blisters act as a sort of cushion. They protect the skin beneath them. You might be tempted to break the blisters, but don't do it! If you pop a blister, it can easily become infected. For this reason, try not to wear clothing that rubs against the blisters.

Second-degree burns heal after a few weeks. The

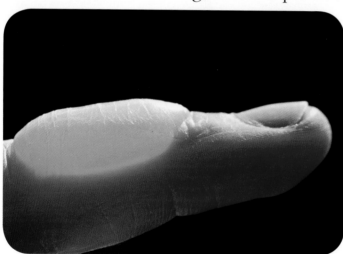

Don't pop your blisters. New skin will form under them and the fluid in the blister will just be absorbed.

body no longer needs the dead skin that formed the blisters. The dead skin peels away and leaves fresh new skin where the burn was.

Third-degree burns are the most serious burns. A third-degree burn destroys the epidermis and

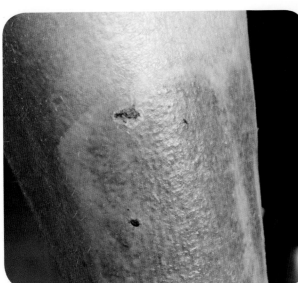

Third-degree burns do not hurt because the skin's nerve endings are destroyed. However, the area around the burn can be very painful.

the entire dermis. With a third-degree burn, the skin often swells up. It may look dry and leathery, too. The burned area may be blue, brown, white, or yellow.

You might be surprised to learn that third-degree burns do not hurt. There's a reason. All the **nerve**

endings in the burned area are destroyed. They can't send pain messages to the brain.

Third-degree burns do not heal the same way first- and second-degree burns do. The skin is extremely damaged, so new skin doesn't form on its own. Instead, doctors often use **skin grafts** on third-degree burns. In an operating room they cover the burned area with a piece of unburned skin from another part of the body.

Your skin has lots of important jobs to do. It holds together the inside of your body. Your skin also protects you from heat, light, and infections. Take good care of your skin. Keep it healthy, and don't let it get burned.

HAVE FUN IN THE SUN— LEARN NOT TO BURN!

Don't use sunscreen just at the beach. Put it on any time you're planning to be outside. Don't forget hard-to-reach areas. Be sure to put sunscreen on the back of your neck and the rims of your ears. Do you swim or sweat a lot? If so, reapply your sunscreen every two hours. Make sure to use sunscreen with an SPF of 15 or greater.

How Does It Happen?

You hear that someone's been burned. What comes to mind? Do you picture a blazing building? Do you imagine a scene with fire trucks, hoses, and ladders?

Many people have been burned or killed in house fires. But you don't have to be trapped in a burning building to get burned. Burns happen in lots of other ways, too. Did you know that burns are a leading cause of accidental injuries at home? Sadly, young people are often the ones who get hurt.

HOW DO KIDS GET BURNED?

As you know, there are different kinds of burns. Children often get **thermal burns**. Thermal burns happen when something hot touches the skin. Scalding is an example of this type of burn. In fact, scalding is the most common type of burn injury among children. It can happen easily enough. A parent turns his or her head for a second, and a toddler reaches for a coffee cup. The hot liquid spills, and the child is scalded.

Scalding occurs in other ways as well. It often happens when a young child is left alone in the bathtub. The child turns on the faucet, and hot water flows into the tub. The child can be badly scalded.

Thermal burns also happen when someone comes in direct contact with a flame or a very hot object. Imagine grabbing a hot pot handle on the stove without using a pot holder. Ouch! That can cause a painful thermal burn. It also hurts to get accidentally burned by a hot curling iron or a match.

When you're cooking, pay attention to what you're doing. It's easy to get burned.

Another type of burn is a **chemical burn**. Chemical burns happen when a strong **acid** or other dangerous substance comes into contact with the body. For example, a toddler might get a chemical burn if he accidentally swallows drain cleaner. Chemical burns sometimes happen when students mix chemicals in school science labs.

Dangerous substances should be kept in locked cabinets where very young children can't get to them.

You can't always see chemical and electrical burns, but they can still be very harmful. These burns can injure the inside of your body. Always see a doctor right away if you get a chemical or electrical burn.

Electrical burns happen when a person comes into contact with an electric current. How do kids get these burns? Sometimes toddlers stick a finger into an electrical outlet. Older kids have gotten electrical burns when they climbed utility poles or antennas on a dare. This is dangerous—and foolish—behavior.

The last type of burn is a **radiation burn**. Most of these burns happen when people stay out in the sun too long. Sunburns can be fairly mild or quite serious. Other sources of radiation, such as **X-rays**, can also cause burns.

Help! It Happened to Me

Tonight is pizza night at your house. Your mom just took two delicious pies out of the oven. You can't wait to sink your teeth into a slice, so you grab one off the pan.

Boy, are you sorry you did that! You didn't know the metal was still so hot. When you picked up the pizza, you burned your fingers. Now you're feeling major pain!

Pizza is a tasty treat. Make sure the pan has cooled before you go for your slice. Getting burned is never fun.

Okay, you have a burn. Don't panic. Do you know what to do? Pick one of these choices:

     A. put butter on the burn

     B. put an ice cube on the burn

     C. run cool water over the burn

Was your answer C? If so, you got it right!

In the past, people used to think you should put butter on a burn. This should never be done. It can cause the burn to get infected. People also used to put ice or very cold water on burns. But that can damage the skin even more. The burn may take longer to heal, too.

What else should you do? It depends on how bad the burn is. If you get burned, it's always best to get an adult to help you. But what if you're home alone? Then you need to know what to do to help yourself.

In the case of a minor burn from a hot object, you should run cool water over the burn for ten to fifteen minutes. Another

Run cool water over a burn. Do not stick your hand in the freezer. That's not a smart choice.

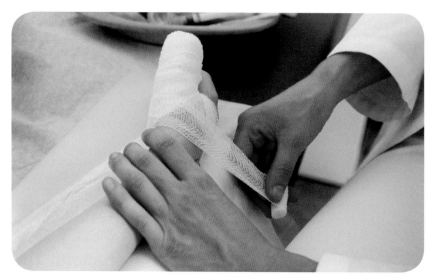

Here a burn is being covered with a gauze bandage after being cleaned and treated.

good choice is to cover the burn with a cool, wet towel. You usually don't have to see a doctor for a minor burn. These burns normally heal on their own.

WHEN IT'S WORSE

Second-degree burns need more care. You should see your doctor as soon as possible. The doctor will clean the burn area and apply an **antibiotic cream**. This helps protect you from infection. Before you leave, the doctor will also cover the burn with a clean **gauze** bandage.

Depending on how serious your second-degree burn is, you might need more treatment. You may have to go back to your doctor's office for further cleaning and bandage changes. You might have to change your bandage at home, too.

THIRD-DEGREE BURNS

No one should ever try to treat a third-degree burn at home. This is especially important if the burn covers a large part of the body. Call for emergency help immediately. While waiting for help to come, cover the burned area with a clean, dry sheet. If you get a third-degree burn, you'll probably have to stay in the hospital. You might need surgery and skin grafts.

WATCH OUT! THAT SLIDE MAY BE HOT!

Are you going to the playground on a really hot day? Be careful. Metal playground equipment, such as slides, can get really hot in the sun. Don't get burned. Try going to the playground in the early morning or late afternoon, when it's cooler. Carefully touch the equipment before using it.

Get Safety Smart

Question: What's better than knowing how to treat a burn?
Answer: Not getting burned at all!

Burn injuries may be common among kids, but there's some good news, too. Many times, burns don't have to happen. Did you know that three-quarters of all burn injuries in children could have been prevented? You can learn ways to stay safe. It's all about becoming safety smart.

CAREFUL COOKING

Are you old enough to cook? If so, then you're old enough to cook carefully. Watch what you wear when using the stove. Never put on baggy clothing or loose long sleeves. These can easily catch on fire. Also, never take anything out of the oven without an oven mitt. Microwave ovens can make things really hot, really fast. So remember to use an oven mitt with this type of oven, too.

Use a pot holder to take pots off the stove as well. It's also helpful to turn pot handles toward the center of the stove. This lessens the chance of someone bumping into a pan and knocking it off the stove.

Are your younger brothers and sisters nearby when you cook? If so, you need to be extra careful.

This girl uses oven mitts to take something out of the oven. Her friend is safety smart too. She's staying a safe distance from the oven.

Use only the stove's back burners if other people are around. Otherwise, a curious little kid might reach for a pot and pull it off the stove. This can result in a very bad burn.

NOT EVERYTHING IS A TOY

Some games are both fun and safe. Others are just plain dangerous. Avoid games that involve matches or cigarette lighters. There are safer ways to have fun. Try not to play near a fireplace or a wood-burning stove, either. It's easy to get burned that way.

People celebrate holidays in different ways. Firecrackers and sparklers are popular and legal in some areas, but many kids have been burned while playing with fire. Don't handle them unless a trusted adult is with you.

Fireworks and sparklers should never be lit indoors. They are for outdoor use only.

WATER WORRIES

Do you use a curling iron or a hair dryer? If so, keep them away from the sink and bathtub. If either of these items falls into the water, never reach in to remove it. The power could pass through the water and into your body. You probably would not survive. Unplug the appliance instead. And don't even think about using an electrical appliance while you are taking a bath.

AN ESCAPE PLAN

No one wants to be in a house fire. But what if a fire happened? Could you safely escape?

Fire spreads quickly. In less than a minute a small fire can turn into a major blaze. A house can soon fill up with thick, black smoke.

That's why you need to make an escape plan ahead of time. Think of two ways you could leave each room in your home. What if the door to the room were blocked by fire or smoke? Maybe you could get out through a window. Make sure your windows aren't stuck shut. Also, learn how to remove a screen quickly in case you need to.

If a fire breaks out, leave the home right away. Don't stop to get your toys, books, or other items. Everything can be replaced but you.

Smoke can be as harmful as fire. What if you have to escape from your home through a smoky area? Drop to your knees and crawl. This makes it easier for you to breathe, because smoke rises. Also, cover your mouth as you leave.

Talk to your family about fire prevention. Ask if all the

Every home should have one smoke detector on each floor. They save thousands of lives each year.

DON'T BE TOO QUICK TO OPEN THAT DOOR

Let's say your home is on fire.
You need to get out, but you've come to a
closed door. Don't open it right away. First, touch it with
the back of your hand. Does the door feel hot? It if does,
the fire is very close by. Use your second escape route
instead. A nearby window might be a safer
choice in this case.

smoke alarms in your home are working. Ask your family
to plan fire drills at home, too. Also make sure you have a fire
extinguisher in your home.

Take pride in knowing how to stay safe. Practice the tips
you've learned in this book. Tell your friends about them too.
Most burns result from being careless or not knowing what to
do. Be a safety-smart kid. Always do your best to make sure
you don't get burned.

GLOSSARY

acid — a strong chemical substance that can burn skin

antibiotic cream — a cream used to kill bacteria

chemical burn — a burn that occurs when a strong acid or other chemical substance comes into contact with the body

electrical burns — burns that result from coming in contact with an electric current

gauze — a type of cotton used for bandages

nerve endings — parts of nerves that can sense pain, such as the pain from a burn

radiation burn — a burn caused by the sun or another form of radiation

scald — to burn with a hot liquid or steam

skin grafts — pieces of skin used to surgically cover an area that has been badly burned

thermal burn — burns that occur when a heat source (such as a flame) touches the skin

x-rays — special pictures that allow a doctor to see beneath your skin

FIND OUT MORE

BOOKS

Donahue, Jill Urban. *Contain the Flame: Outdoor Fire Safety*. Minneapolis, MN: Picture Window Books, 2009.

Gray, Susan H. *The Skin*. Mankato, MN: Child's World, 2006.

Llewellyn, Claire. *Hygiene and Health*. Mankato, MN: QED Publications, 2006.

Pancella, Peggy. *Fire Safety*. Chicago: Heinemann, 2005.

DVDS

How and When to Dial 911. Bird Rock Entertainment, 2007.

Lots & Lots of Fire Songs & Safety Tips. Marshall Publishing & Promotions, 2008.

WEBSITES

FireSafety.gov for Kids

www.firesafety.gov/Kids/flash.shtm

Check out this fun site for lots of helpful hints on how to stay burn-free.
Don't miss the crossword puzzles, matching game, and word searches.

Fire Safety for Kids

www.firesafetyforkids.org

Learn more about fire safety through great games on this website. Be
sure to try the Danger Challenge Flash Game and the Word Search links.

NYS Department of State—Fire Safety for Kids

www.dos.state.ny.us/kidsroom/firesafe/firesafe.html
Join Hershey, the arson dog, on a learning adventure to find out
how to escape from a fire.

INDEX

Page numbers in **boldface** are illustrations.

ABOUT THE AUTHOR

Award-winning author Elaine Landau has written more than three hundred books for young readers. Many of them are about health and science.

Landau received a bachelor's degree in English and journalism from New York University and a master's degree in library and information science from Pratt Institute. You can visit Elaine Landau at her website: www.elainelandau.com.